The Secret
to Staying Young

The Secret to Staying Young

www.leesterrey.co.uk

ISBN-13: 978-0-9957565-1-9

Dedicated to all those who care about the little things
that make a big difference.

Effie bounced into her daddy's study, full of beams and smiles. "Guess where we went on a school trip today?" she asked.

"I'm busy doing work with the bank. You know not to disturb me until supper-time," her daddy grumpily replied.

Effie protested, "But Daddy, we went to a Vegan Festival at the care home. Everyone was laughing and smiling. We should take Grandad Reg."

Her daddy put his head in his hands. "Oh Effie, we have been through this. Grandad is happy in Stockport. Besides, he would never leave that cat."

"But," Effie persisted, "he may even be able to bring Mabel with him - Toby's Nana has her cat there. Can we please take him this weekend when he comes to visit... Please?"

Effie's daddy impatiently checked his watch; his Friday deadline to submit his reports was looming and Effie was not going to let this one go. He looked at his daughter's big brown eyes and let out a sigh. "All right. I give in. We can pop in there after we pick Grandad up tomorrow, ok? But you know what he's like. We have tried before and he doesn't want to be a bother to anyone, he's happy where he is."

Effie gave her daddy a big hug. "Thank you! Thank you! Thank you! I just know he will love it there."

The next day, Effie stood hand in hand with Grandad Reg outside a smart-looking building which boasted a large green and white sign that read, 'Barchester, Celebrating Life'.

"Why are we here?" Grandad Reg whispered to Effie. "I'm far too young to go into a home."

Just as she was about to answer, a camper van drove past them filled with people singing loudly, "We're off to see the wizard..." They watched it slowly go over a speed bump, which resulted in a loud cheer from the passengers before they resumed their singing.

"Daddy has arranged for us to look around to see if you might like it," Effie replied. "They have all sorts of fun activities that you can do."

Grandad Reg's bushy grey eyebrows pushed together to form a slight frown and he squinted at her over the top of his glasses.

"You shouldn't worry yourself my dear. I'm ok with my Mabel and the football on the TV. I don't need anything else."

Effie wasn't ready to give up just yet. "Aren't you lonely?" she asked.

"It's a bit quieter these days since the old pub turned into a posh cocktail bar for the youngsters," Grandad agreed.

Effie was about to reply, when the doors to the home opened and a waft of delicious smells passed under their noses, beckoning them into the building.

Grandad Reg took a deep sniff. "Oh. Freshly baked bread! Now that might be worth a look."

"You and your bread," Effie's daddy said. "You haven't baked anything since mum died. Do you even remember how to do it?"

"The day I forget how to bake bread, is the day that I'm an old man." Grandad Reg winked at Effie, "I owned the best bakery in Stockport for 60 years."

A mobile phone started buzzing and Effie's daddy rummaged for it in his pocket. "Arrgh. Why is work calling me on a Saturday? You two go in. I have to take this call."

Inside was a brightly lit, large space that had sofas, tables and chairs. Upbeat radio music was playing in the background and the now stronger smell of delicious baking made their tummies rumble.

They were greeted by a friendly lady. The badge on her cardigan showed her name to be Sue. "You must be Reg. I hope you haven't been waiting long," she said. "Some of the residents were going on an outing to the theatre and we had to make sure they were all safely onto the van. So you've come to look around today?"

"Well, not really..." Grandad Reg started to reply.

"Yes we have," Effie interrupted, "but we need to wait for my daddy. He's talking with work." She pointed outside.

"That's fine. No rush. Please help yourself to tea and coffee. I will get some details for you." As Sue walked back to reception, her phone buzzed and she answered it.

Grandad Reg turned to Effie and with a naughty twinkle in his eye said, "I can smell that bread. Shall we see if we can find it?"

Effie smiled widely. "We'll have to sneak past," she whispered.

They tiptoed past Sue into a corridor, looking for the room where the smell was coming from.

Just as they passed a large brown door with a well-polished brass handle, they heard a shout. "Yeeha!" Followed by stamping.

"What's that?" asked Effie. "It's coming from behind this door."

Grandad Reg opened it and to his surprise saw three ladies dressed as cowboys, stamping, dancing and kicking their legs to music.

"Yeeha!" the lady in the pink dress shouted out again. "Come and join us!"

Grandad let out a gasp. "I can't do that. I'm 81 years old!"

"81?" the lady in green screeched over the top of the music. "Ooh so young! I'll have you know I'm 94 tomorrow! Kick higher, girls!"

"Grandad! She's older than you! But how can she kick so high?" Effie asked loudly over the noise. The lady in pink line-danced across to Effie.

"The... secret to us... staying young... is behind... the... blue... door," she huffed between kicks.

"Let's go and see!" Effie said excitedly and they closed the door, leaving the three ladies laughing and yeehaing.

Effie put her ear to the blue door. "I can't hear anything," she said. She quietly opened the door and there was peace and calm in the room. There were people sitting cross-legged with their hands on their knees and the smell of lavender in the air.

A man at the front of the group balanced his whole body on one finger! He opened an eye and peered at Effie and Grandad Reg. "Do you want to have a go?" he murmured in a low tone.

"I can't do that, I am 81 years old!" Grandad Reg whispered back.

The man opened both eyes and stared at them. "81? That is so young! I'm 95!"

"Grandad, he is older than you! But how can he do that?" Effie asked.

The man pivoted onto another finger and replied, "The secret to us staying young is behind the red door."

"Let's go and see!" Effie said, and gently closed the door.

From behind the red door came the sound of clashing of metal on metal.

"Grandad, I'm not sure that we should open this one," Effie said, worried.

That twinkle appeared again in his eye and Grandad said, "But I would like to know what is causing that sound. Wouldn't you?" He opened the red door and to their amazement they had stepped back into Tudor times. People were dressed in Tudor clothes, and a fierce sword fight was going on between a man and a woman with shoulder length white hair!

With one arm behind her back, the woman yelled at the opposition. "Put your guard up!" She leapt forward and there was another clash of the swords. "I win!" she shouted.

She turned to Grandad and Effie. "Would you like to fight me next?" she asked.

"I can't fight with a sword! I'm 81!" Grandad replied.

"81?" she laughed. "That is so young! I picked up my first sword when I was 96!"

"Grandad, she hadn't done it before she was 96! But how?" Effie asked in wonder.

The woman strutted across to where they stood. "The secret to us staying young is behind the green door," she said proudly. Then she turned to the cheering crowd that had gathered to watch her, and shouted, "Who's next?"

Effie and Grandad looked at each other in amazement. "I think we should find out what's behind the green door," Effie said.

The green door was being kept slightly ajar by a glinting, shining object.

"I wonder what a spanner's doing down there?" Grandad said out loud.

"Shall we see?" asked Effie.

They opened the door to find a very fine-looking gentleman in full WWII uniform cleaning underneath the wing of a very large plane.

"That's a Lancaster bomber!" Grandad exclaimed. "My brother flew those in the war!"

At the sound of voices, the gentleman looked up. "Your brother was in the war?" he called out. Effie noticed a slight northern tone to his accent, similar to Grandad's. The gentleman marched across to them with a stern look on his face.

"Yes, he was based in Sheffield," replied Grandad with pride.

The gentleman's face softened into a smile. "What a coincidence! I was based there too. We must swap stories! I have just fixed this plane and I'm about to clean it. Would you like to help?"

"I can't clean a plane! I'm 81!" Grandad replied.

"81! That is so young. I can climb that ladder over there and I'm 97!" the gentleman exclaimed.

"Grandad, he is older than you and he can still climb a ladder! But how?" Effie wondered.

The tall man stooped low over Effie. He tapped his nose and said, "Aha, little lady. The secret to us staying young is behind the yellow door."

With that he promptly turned on his heel and marched back to the plane.

Bushy eyebrows raised in surprise, Grandad said, "Let's take a look."

Effie and Grandad heard a swishing noise as they approached the yellow door. Effie bent down and pulled at a long piece of straw that was poking underneath.

"Why would a room full of straw keep them young?" Effie asked.

Grandad Reg shrugged his shoulders. They opened the door to find a beautiful silver coloured horse with large brown eyes and a long flowing mane gently taking carrots from a small lady with wispy white hair and a face filled with joy.

Effie gasped in awe.

"Would you like to feed him?" the lady asked in a quiet well-spoken voice.

"The biggest animal I've ever fed in my life is my cat, Mabel!" Grandad replied. "I've never fed a horse before and I'm too old to start now."

The lady's reply was sweet and soft. "I'm 98 and if I can do it so can you. If you like cats ..." She beckoned Grandad Reg in closer and gently tapped his hand, "Then the secret to us staying young is behind the white door." She picked up another carrot and held it to the horse's velvety muzzle, as it waited patiently for its next treat.

The horse whinnied gently as Effie and Grandad left the room.

"There are only two more doors," said Effie as she opened the white door.

Inside they were greeted with a sight that filled both of their hearts with joy. In the centre of the room sat a lady in an armchair. She was surrounded by cats!

The lady let out a little chuckle as the cats' silky fur brushed against her skin. "Oh, they're so soft!" she said. She picked one up and gave it a huge cuddle. The cat let out a loud purr and bumped its head on the lady's chin, trying to get more attention.

"Hello dear! You're looking very well." she said to Grandad.

Grandad seemed lost for words. After a moment he said, "I have a cat called Mabel".

"I just love cats," the lady replied. "They remind me of when I was a little girl. I might be 99 years old, but they keep me young."

"I feel the same way about freshly baked bread," said Grandad. Effie noticed that his face clouded over. Then he added sadly, "I haven't had that for a while though."

The lady let out a joyous laugh that made the cats on her lap jump with surprise. "In that case, you need to go through the doors at the end of the corridor."

After they left the room, Effie watched her Grandad. His face was sad and he seemed lost in his own thoughts, as if he was remembering better times gone by.

Celebrating life

"Grandad, shall we find out what's behind this last door?" she asked, and took his large hand into hers.

Grandad smiled at Effie and the twinkle returned to his eye. "Yes, come on!"

When they stepped through the door, they found themselves in a beautiful large garden with trees and flowers. People dressed in grass skirts were dancing to music being played on steel drums. There were tables covered in brightly coloured baskets, holding lots of scrumptious looking fruit and vegetables for the residents and their guests.

They had stepped into a Caribbean party!

At that moment, Effie's daddy appeared from behind a tree wearing flower necklaces and coconuts. He led a long line of conga dancers behind him, all cheering to the music.

Effie and Grandad stood open-mouthed at this spectacular scene.

"I thought I was too old to go to the Caribbean!" Grandad laughed out loud.

A young lady dressed in a sumo-wrestling suit bounced in front of them. "You don't have to go to the Caribbean to experience it, we bring it to you, anything can happen here," she said, as another person in a sumo wrestling suit bumped into her and they both fell to the floor laughing.

"Look Grandad! Look!" shouted Effie, and she pointed to the table that had a centre-piece full of different types of freshly baked bread.

Grandad picked up a piece and took in its smell, "Now, this is what keeps me young."

"I don't understand, how does it keep you young?" Effie asked.

"It reminds me of the day I met my beautiful wife. Your Nana. She came into my bakery and I fell in love with her the moment I saw her."

"Reg, there you are!" called Sue as she walked over to them. "I thought I had lost you!"

"We weren't lost! We saw so many people having adventures," Grandad laughed back.

Then he turned to Effie and said, "I think I'm ready to start my own adventure here too. Don't you?"

Effie beamed her biggest smile yet. "Does that mean you are going to stay?"

Grandad took his precious grand-daughter into his arms and gave her a big squeeze.

"Yes, Effie, it's time," he replied as the conga dancers led by Effie's daddy paraded past them.

The secret to staying young:

Try something new...

share stories with friends,

surround yourself with things you love...

and of course, eat freshly baked bread.

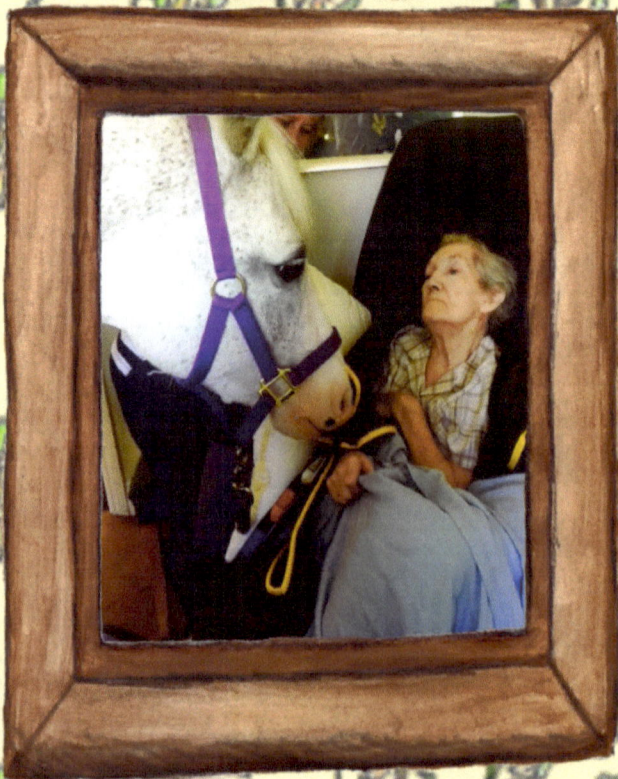

Buddy

ARTISTS

Imogen Bailey
Caitlin Beresford
Erin Craddock
Eleanor Dean
Adam Freemantle
Grace Gardener
Laurie Glen
Elysia Griffiths
Hannah Hedley
Mollie Johnson

Georgia Lane
Emily Lindsay
Tom Mitchell
Isobel O'Rourke
Eleanor Prime
Freya Rippington
Jack Smith
Ashley Syron
Jakub Wozniak

A note from the Author: Lee Sterrey

The inspiration behind this story came from the amazing activities team led by Hannah Mulholland, who works at Harper Fields Care Home in Warwickshire.

Each of the 'rooms' was inspired by something that the team had achieved. For example, they really did get a horse into a resident's bedroom as it was one of her deepest wishes to feed a horse again, but she was too poorly to go outside.

The team provide many wide ranging experiences, everything from multiple trips per week to theatres, parks and museums, through to bringing the Caribbean to their lawns in Warwickshire!

The activities that residents undertake sometimes unlock memories of hidden pastimes. On a trip to ThinkTank (Birmingham) a resident shared his experiences of flying a Lancaster Bomber in WWII. This sharing of experiences helps the team to create new connections and have deeper, more meaningful conversations.

Residents with memory loss may not remember volunteering themselves to have a sword fight at Mary Arden's Farm, but they return to the care home content that they had a good time. It's this emotional connection that the team at Harper Fields goes to incredible lengths to achieve, to provide their residents with new experiences and most importantly, help them to feel happy.

The home is supported by a whole host of volunteers, but in particular, Elizabeth Scott deserves a special mention as she brings her show cats in on a weekly basis to provide 'Pet Therapy' sessions. It's a firm favourite with the residents and the cats enjoy the pampering as well.

This book was supported by the wonderful talents of the pupils at Heart of England School who donated their time and over 150 pictures to bring this story to life. A special thanks goes to Lydia Mulholland, their art teacher, who inspired the pupils on their creativity.

About Lee Sterrey
In addition to writing about adventures that happen on her small farm, Lee creates 'community books' which involve many pieces of art from school children.

www.leesterrey.co.uk

www.ingramcontent.com/pod-product-compliance
Lightning Source LLC
Chambersburg PA
CBHW040020050426
42452CB00002B/57